CW01512604

Original title:

Kaleidoscopic Whispers Beside the Dragon Lawn

Author: Kene Elistrand

ISBN HARDBACK: 978-1-80559-240-2

ISBN PAPERBACK: 978-1-80559-739-1

Patterns of Light Through the Canopy

Sunlight filters down with grace,
Leaves whisper secrets, a warm embrace.
Shadows dance on the forest floor,
Nature's artwork forevermore.

Birds flit by, their wings aglow,
A symphony of colors in vibrant flow.
Every branch a painter's brush,
Nature's beauty in every hush.

Moss carpets the ground, soft and deep,
In this serene place, the world can sleep.
Flickers of gold and emerald green,
In the heart of the woods, a tranquil scene.

The breeze carries stories untold,
Of ancient trees and spirits bold.
In this sacred space, wonder ignites,
Patterns of light, enchanting sights.

As dusk approaches, shadows expand,
Nature's canvas, both vast and grand.
The canopy whispers a soft goodbye,
In glowing hues, the day does die.

The Serpent's Song in a Technicolor Realm

In a world where colors collide,
A serpent glides with grace and pride.
Vibrant scales like a rainbow's thread,
In this realm, the wild are fed.

With a flick of its tongue, it sings,
Echoes of magic the twilight brings.
Every note a shimmering light,
Dancing shadows in the night.

The trees embrace the melody,
Leaves sway to the harmonious decree.
In every corner, beauty resounds,
A spellbound symphony, nature abounds.

Stars begin to twinkle and gleam,
Reflecting the serpent's enchanting dream.
In twilight's grasp, the colors bloom,
Spreading joy, dispelling gloom.

As the night deepens, colors merge,
A flow of brilliance begins to surge.
In this vibrant world, the serpent leads,
Painting dreams, fulfilling needs.

Celestial Reflections on the Meadow's Edge

In the meadow where the wildflowers sway,
The sky blushes as night greets day.
Stars emerge, a twinkling crowd,
Their beauty whispered, soft and loud.

Mirrored in the stillness of the pond,
Reflections dance, of life beyond.
Every ripple tells a tale,
Of cosmic wonders on the trail.

Crickets chirp in a soothing tune,
Underneath the watchful moon.
Gentle breezes brush the grass,
In this moment, time does pass.

Fireflies flicker, like stars on earth,
Celebrating life, love, and mirth.
In this meadow, peace ignites,
Celestial magic in the nights.

As dawn approaches with golden light,
The meadow awakens, pure delight.
Nature's canvas, a splendid sight,
Celestial wonders, shining bright.

Harmonies of Hues in Twilight's Grip

When day dips low and shadows grow,
A tapestry of hues begins to show.
Soft pastel whispers fill the sky,
As daylight bids the world goodbye.

Lilac, orange, and cerulean blend,
Twilight's palette, a magical trend.
With each stroke, the world ignites,
Harmonies of hues in tranquil nights.

The wind carries secrets from afar,
Guided by the glow of the evening star.
Nature's song sings sweet and clear,
In this moment, the heart draws near.

As night unfolds, the colors fade,
Yet memories of beauty aren't betrayed.
Each twilight tells a timeless lore,
A dance of shades forevermore.

In the stillness, the world finds peace,
Under the cosmos, wonders never cease.
In twilight's grip, dreams take flight,
Harmonies of hues embrace the night.

Luminous Dreams on the Garden Path

Soft whispers float on the evening air,
Petals shimmering, without a care.
Moonlight glimmers on dewdrop kings,
A dance of shadows; the nightingale sings.

Beneath the arching boughs so wide,
Dreams unfold where secrets hide.
Each step echoes, hearts align,
In this garden, pure and divine.

Twinkling stars in the azure sky,
Guide weary souls as they wander by.
With every breath, a story spun,
Luminous dreams melt into one.

The fragrant air sings ancient songs,
In this haven, where each heart belongs.
A tapestry woven with threads of light,
In the garden's embrace, everything feels right.

Come tread softly on the sacred ground,
Where every heartbeat can be found.
In luminous dreams, hopes arise,
The garden path never lies.

Dance of the Multihued Mirage

On the horizon, colors swirl and blend,
A vibrant dance that knows no end.
Mirages beckon, inviting the soul,
In rhythmic waves, they make us whole.

Whispers of amber and shades of blue,
In every moment, the world feels new.
With a flick of light, the shadows play,
A mosaic of dreams, brightening the day.

Footsteps echo on the golden sand,
Where visions flicker, held in hand.
The dance of colors, a sight so rare,
In the mirage's arms, we lose our care.

Beneath the skies, a symphony pours,
Each heartbeat steps through open doors.
We chase the light, we ride the tide,
In the multihued world's endless stride.

As day turns to dusk, we weave and spin,
The dance continues, forever begins.
With laughter and love, we find our place,
In the heart of the mirage, a warm embrace.

Flickering Sirens in the Green Haven

Amidst the woods where the wild things sing,
Flickering lights, like tiny wings.
A symphony whispers through the trees,
Each note a treasure carried by the breeze.

Sirens beckon from shadows deep,
Promises stirring, secrets to keep.
With every rustle, enchantments flow,
In the green haven, magic starts to grow.

Beneath the boughs, soft laughter dwells,
The heart's stories that nature tells.
A journey begun in the dappled shade,
With flickering sirens, we're unafraid.

Sunlight dances on leaves that sway,
Guiding our hearts as they drift away.
Within the glade, we find our truth,
In the flickering glow, we renew our youth.

The echoes linger, the evening calls,
Through winding paths, our spirit falls.
In the green haven, we shall remain,
Flickering sirens, forever our refrain.

Secrets Beneath the Moth-Hued Sky

Beneath a canopy of pastel light,
Secrets linger in the fading sight.
Moths flutter softly, weaving tales,
As twilight whispers, the evening exhales.

Shadows lengthen in gentle hues,
Every corner hides vibrant news.
In the hush, stories intertwine,
Beneath the sky, soft and divine.

With every breath, the past invites,
Lurking memories of lost delights.
In the moth's wings, the truth unfolds,
Secrets beckon, a tale retold.

Drifting softly on the evening's breeze,
Hearts awaken, enchanted, at ease.
In twilight's embrace, we search to find,
The magic hidden, not far behind.

Beneath the stars where silence reigns,
The secret garden softly gains.
In moth-hued skies, we start to dream,
Unraveling life's exquisite theme.

Shadows Playing Beneath Celestial Canopies

Shadows dance in twilight's gleam,
Beneath the stars, a silver dream.
Whispers weave through ancient trees,
Where nightingale sings soft as breeze.

Moonlight glistens on the brook,
Nature's tale in every nook.
Fingers trace the path of light,
In a world that feels just right.

Crickets play their nighttime song,
While the shadows glide along.
Secret stories left unspoken,
In the silence, hearts are woven.

Glimmers twirl in gentle grace,
Embraced by night's warm, soft embrace.
Through the dark, such beauty sways,
In the realm where magic plays.

All beneath the sky's vast dome,
In shadows, we find our true home.
Stars above will always shine,
Guiding us through realms divine.

Tints of Twilight in the Secret Garden

In the garden, colors blend,
As daylight starts to end.
Petals bloom in muted light,
Whispering secrets of the night.

Lavender skies caress the ground,
While the evening's breath is found.
Softly painting dusk with grace,
Each shadow finds its perfect place.

Silhouettes of leaves in flight,
Dance with fireflies, pure delight.
In the hush, a promise grows,
Of dreams that blossom like a rose.

Beneath the arch of twilight's dome,
Every heart can find its home.
Nature whispers, gently calls,
In secret gardens, magic sprawls.

Colors fade but never cease,
In the garden, find your peace.
Embrace the night, let worries part,
As twilight dances in your heart.

Harmonic Threads of Nature's Puzzle

Nature sings in vibrant sound,
Harmony in every round.
Threads of life entwine and weave,
In the tapestry we believe.

Mountains echo with the breeze,
Rustling leaves upon the trees.
Every creature plays a note,
In this symphony, we float.

Rivers flow with timeless grace,
Reflecting light in nature's face.
Each petal, each stone, a part,
Of the music in our heart.

Seasons shift, yet still we feel,
The harmony of earth's appeal.
In the silence, hear the call,
Nature's song connects us all.

With every dusk and every dawn,
In this puzzle, we belong.
Threads of life will pull us near,
As we listen, always clear.

The Flicker of Hope in Colorful Glades

In the glades where colors breathe,
Hope ignites like autumn leaves.
Sunlight filters through the trees,
Wrapping hearts with gentle ease.

Petals lean towards the light,
In the dance of day and night.
Every glimmer holds a dream,
In the flow of nature's stream.

Butterflies with wings of grace,
Paint the air in soft embrace.
In each flutter, hope is found,
Whispers echo all around.

As the shadows stretch and sway,
Love and light will find a way.
In every hue, a story bright,
Guiding souls through darkest night.

Embrace the glade, feel the spark,
Flickers bright, dispelling dark.
In these moments, hearts align,
Finding joy in nature's design.

Palette of Dreams in the Meadow's Murmurs

In the meadow, whispers play,
Colors burst in bright array.
Petals dance with gentle grace,
Nature's heart finds its place.

Sunlight weaves through gentle blades,
Crafting dreams in leafy shades.
Butterflies, with wings so light,
Flit through day, ignite the night.

Laughter lingers in the breeze,
Painting skies with swaying trees.
Each flower shares a story dear,
Murmurs soft for all to hear.

Clouds drift past in soft embrace,
Reflecting joys, the world's grace.
Moments captured, fleeting, sweet,
In the meadow, hearts can meet.

Tales of Color Interwoven in Darkness

In shadows deep, where secrets weave,
Colors twine, refusing to leave.
Whispers blend in midnight hue,
Crafting tales both old and new.

Crimson threads in velvet night,
Stitching dreams with quiet light.
Emerald eyes of night unveiled,
Story's pulse, though faint, prevailed.

Glimmers dance on silver streams,
Capturing the heart of dreams.
Every murmur softly speaks,
Of journeys taken, paths unique.

Mysterious forms in shrouded space,
Find their rhythm, set their pace.
Together in the dark they find,
A canvas born of soul and mind.

Celestial Paths Through Verdant Wonderland

Underneath a cosmic sky,
Paths of green and dreams fly high.
Stars adorn the leaves with grace,
In this wonder, time finds space.

Winding trails through emerald maze,
Nature's beauty, a lasting praise.
Moonlight kisses each fresh bloom,
Making night a soft perfume.

Gentle fauna roam with glee,
Welcoming the night so free.
Every rustle sings a tune,
Guided by the silver moon.

Through the woods, the starlight weaves,
Whispering of countless leaves.
In this realm where dreams reside,
Hearts entwined, with hope as guide.

Harmonizing Shadows of Flora and Fauna

In the twilight, shadows blend,
Flora and fauna, hand in hand.
Herbs whisper secrets as they sway,
Crafting harmony in their play.

Creatures dart through dense embrace,
Finding joy in nature's space.
Rhythms pulse beneath the ground,
Nature's music, sweetly found.

Flowers bloom where shadows drape,
In their midst, the dreams escape.
Colors dance on branches high,
Painting stories in the sky.

Each petal, leaf, and feathered flight,
Melding softly into night.
Together crafting songs so pure,
In the dark, they shall endure.

Celestial Flickers in Woodland Dreams

In the hush of twilight's veil,
Stars begin their gentle tale.
Moonlight dances on the stream,
A world wrapped in silver dream.

Whispers rustle through the trees,
Carried softly by the breeze.
Fireflies flit in joyful play,
As night stretches to greet the day.

Leaves shimmer with a secret glow,
Lighting paths where few would go.
Nature's lullaby so sweet,
Guides the wanderers' tired feet.

Branches weave a tapestry,
Of magic held in harmony.
Crickets serenade the night,
While shadows dance in soft moonlight.

Celestial flickers near and far,
Tell of dreams beneath the stars.
In this woodland, time stands still,
By the heart's enchanting will.

Serpent's Flight Across a Technicolor Sky

A serpent slips through hues of gold,
Across a canvas bold and cold.
Its scales reflect the sunset's fire,
In silent grace, it climbs up higher.

Clouds gather like a painted stream,
Each motion shapes a vibrant dream.
With every twist and every turn,
The sky ignites, the colors burn.

In this dance of light and shade,
The serpent's path begins to fade.
Yet still it glides through liquid skies,
Where every breath is quick with sighs.

Textures blend in wild delight,
As day falls, yielding to the night.
The colors bleed, a sweet collide,
The serpent's flight, an endless ride.

Reflections shimmer, bold and bright,
Across this overwhelming sight.
Nature's palette paints the air,
With every scale, a whispered prayer.

Chasing Light Through the Labyrinth of Leaves

Beneath the boughs, a path unfolds,
Where sunlight weaves through tales untold.
A labyrinth of emerald close,
Hides treasures only light can expose.

Shadows stretch in vibrant greens,
Where time loses its silent means.
I chase the spark through twisting trails,
Finding joy where wonder prevails.

Each rustling leaf, a promise near,
Of stories whispered to the ear.
Guided by the sun's warm glow,
I wander where the wild things grow.

Branches arch, a cathedral's dome,
In nature's heart, I've found my home.
The light, a guide through tangled ways,
Illuminates the heart's deep maze.

In this embrace of leaf and light,
All worries fade, the spirit's flight.
Through nature's maze, forever free,
Chasing light, I simply be.

Refracted Whispers of the Sylvan Glade

In the glade where shadows play,
Sunlight stretches, bright and gay.
Refracted whispers in the air,
Speak of beauty, rich and rare.

Mossy carpets underfoot,
Are soft like dreams, and all are rooted.
Ferns unfurl with every sigh,
While butterflies drift gently by.

Cool streams murmur tales of old,
Where secrets linger, sweet and bold.
Nature's echoes fill the space,
With every ripple, every trace.

Gentle breezes weave their song,
In this glade where all belong.
Each branch a note, each leaf a beat,
In harmony, our hearts do meet.

Refracted whispers all around,
In every corner, peace is found.
In sylvan magic, dreams arise,
Underneath these sprawling skies.

Luminous Dialogues in Nature's Sanctuary

Whispers of wind, soft and light,
Secrets shared in morning's bright.
Trees sway gently, branches entwine,
Nature speaks in rhythm divine.

Sunlight filters through the leaves,
A tapestry that gently weaves.
Birdsong lingers, sweet and clear,
Echoes of the forest near.

Footsteps tread on mossy ground,
In this haven, peace is found.
Every petal, every stone,
Tells a tale of nature's own.

Clouds drift lazily overhead,
Casting dreams on paths we tread.
Rustling grasses, soft and low,
Guide us where the wild things grow.

In this sanctuary, hearts align,
As nature's wonders intertwine.
In luminous dialogues, we engage,
Turning each page, a timeless stage.

The Magical Ebb of Vibrant Reflections

Ripples dance on water's face,
Colors swirling, finding grace.
With each wave, a story flows,
Magic hides where the river goes.

Beneath the bridge, shadows play,
Nature draws a bright display.
Reflections shimmer, light cascades,
Creating worlds where silence wades.

Sunsets blaze in shades of gold,
Mysteries in twilight told.
Every ripple tells a tale,
Echoes of a dreamlike sail.

The moonrise bright, a silver stream,
Woven into nature's dream.
Stars appear, a twinkling show,
As night whispers secrets low.

In these moments, time stands still,
Capturing hearts with every thrill.
In vibrant reflections, we unite,
A magical ebb in the heart of night.

Dance of the Leaves in a Colorful Reverie

In the breeze, the leaves take flight,
Spinning softly in golden light.
Autumn blushes, colors blaze,
Nature's canvas, a vibrant maze.

Each leaf twirls, a graceful spin,
Whispers of change, old and thin.
Crimson, amber, ochre bright,
A symphony of pure delight.

Gathering to the earth below,
Whispering secrets only they know.
A blanket soft with colors strewn,
Dancing together beneath the moon.

The rustle sings a playful tune,
As shadows lengthen, afternoon.
In this reverie, hearts can soar,
United with the earth once more.

Nature gathers, all take part,
In this dance, we share a heart.
A colorful reverie so sweet,
Where every moment feels complete.

Enigmatic Shades Beneath Hanging Ferns

In cool shadows, secrets lie,
Where ferns reach out to touch the sky.
Mysterious shapes dance and play,
Enigmatic shades of green and gray.

Droplets cling to leafy tips,
Nature's jewels on gentle slips.
Kissed by mist in morning's light,
A hidden realm of pure delight.

Paths untrodden, softly worn,
Lead us to where dreams are born.
Roots embrace the earth with care,
Whispering wisdom everywhere.

Amongst the ferns, time fades away,
Lost in wonder, we choose to stay.
Every rustle, every sigh,
Holds a magic that will never die.

In nature's hold, our spirits blend,
Where every moment can transcend.
Enigmatic shades softly call,
Beneath the ferns, we find it all.

The Spectrum of Silence Beneath the Sun

In whispers soft, the shadows play,
A canvas bright where dreams hold sway.
The sun dips low, the day reclaims,
Each sigh of night, a whispered name.

Beneath the glow, the silence reigns,
In echoes lost, the heart sustains.
Nature breathes in colors bold,
A symphony, a tale untold.

Mountains cradle the fading light,
While stars awaken, bold and bright.
In twilight's hush, the world comes near,
A tapestry where thoughts appear.

With open hearts and open eyes,
We wander where the silence lies.
Beneath the sun, our spirits dance,
In gentle waves of fate and chance.

Radiant Footprints in the Garden's Whisper

In gardens green where secrets bloom,
Each footstep leads to hidden room.
Petals sigh as breezes play,
In nature's heart, we find our way.

The sunlight spills on leaves so bright,
Guiding paths with gentle light.
Footprints soft on earthy bed,
In silence, all our dreams are fed.

Each flower holds a tale revered,
A whisper of the love we've steered.
With every breath, the world unfolds,
In colors rich, our lives retold.

In stillness, hear the garden speak,
A melody, both bold and meek.
Through vibrant hues, our spirits soar,
In nature's grasp, we are much more.

Sunlit Reveries in a Dreamer's Grove

In groves of gold where sunlight spills,
A dreamer's heart the moment fills.
With shadows deep beneath the trees,
The whispers dance upon the breeze.

Time pauses here, in golden hue,
Each thought a song, each dream a clue.
In gentle sways of branches high,
We paint our stories in the sky.

Ethereal visions come alive,
In realms where fantasy does thrive.
The sunlit paths, they twirl and bend,
In every heartbeat, worlds transcend.

Together lost in reverie,
Nature cradles our mystery.
With open minds, we find our place,
In sunlit dreams, through time and space.

Colors Intertwined in Nature's Embrace

In vibrant hues where earth adorns,
Each color blooms as daylight warms.
With petals bright in soft caress,
Nature weaves a tapestry blessed.

From azure skies to emerald fields,
A symphony of life it yields.
In every shade, a heartbeat lies,
Reflecting passion in our eyes.

The sunset weaves in orange and pink,
While flowers dance and rivers wink.
In harmony, each shade entwines,
Together painting life's designs.

Oh, nature's brush, both bold and grand,
With gentle strokes, we understand.
In every moment, beauty thrives,
In colors bright, our spirit strives.

Serene Harmony of Colors in Drifted Dreams

In twilight's calm, colors blend,
Whispers of peace, the night shall send.
Dreams drift softly, beneath the stars,
Each hue a tale, from near to far.

Gentle streams reflect the sky,
Where the pastel dreams softly lie.
A tapestry of silence spun,
In harmony, all hearts are one.

Petals dance on a soft breeze,
Swaying lightly among the trees.
In every shadow, light finds space,
An evening's touch, a soft embrace.

Beneath the moon's tender light,
Colors mingle, a beautiful sight.
Each moment a serene delight,
In drifted dreams, the heart takes flight.

Together in this painted night,
We find solace, joy, and light.
With every breath, a canvas drawn,
As colors wake with the dawn.

Tales of the Vibrant Wilderness Untold

In jungles deep, secrets reside,
With colors vibrant, nature's pride.
Each leaf and flower, a story spun,
In wild embrace, life has begun.

Whiskers twitch of creatures small,
In the brush, they hear the call.
A chorus rises, both fierce and sweet,
In wilderness, all paths meet.

Mountains tower, bold and grand,
While rivers carve through the land.
In thickets thick and skies so wide,
The tales are rich, where dreams abide.

Rustling leaves share whispered lore,
Of ancient times and much more.
In each shadow, a memory waits,
Of vibrant life beyond the gates.

With every step, the stories blend,
In nature's heart, where life won't end.
Tales of wild, fierce and bold,
In vibrant wilderness, dreams unfold.

Enchanted Conversations in Lush Shadows

In quiet groves where secrets dwell,
The breeze carries a fragrant spell.
Leaves converse in whispers low,
In lush shadows, their tales flow.

Moonlight dances on silky ferns,
As nature shares its many turns.
A nightingale sings sweet and clear,
In every note, a voice we hear.

Magic weaves through tangled vines,
In every twist, a spark that shines.
Gentle kisses of wind and dusk,
In every heart, a softened husk.

Beetles hum in twilight's glow,
While fireflies put on a show.
Within this realm of quiet cheer,
Conversations bloom, sincere and near.

In enchanted stillness, hearts align,
With nature's rhythm, a love divine.
In lush shadows, where dreams commence,
Life unfolds in a silent dance.

Swaying Colors of Graceful Breezes

In fields of gold where wildflowers sway,
Colors dance beneath the rays.
Each petal whispers to the wind,
In graceful breezes, hearts rescind.

The azure sky, an endless sea,
In every hue, we find we're free.
Clouds drift softly, tales of their own,
In nature's brush, beauty's shown.

A symphony of vibrant shades,
In every corner, a memory fades.
With every gust, a story shared,
In swaying colors, hearts have bared.

Gentle rustle of greens untold,
In laughter light, moments unfold.
The horizon glows with sunset blush,
As colors mingle, soft and lush.

In twilight's hand, our dreams take flight,
Through every shade, the soul ignites.
In swaying colors, we find a chance,
To join the world in nature's dance.

Quirky Shadows in the Serpent's Embrace

Beneath the shade where secrets dwell,
A serpent coils, casting a spell.
With flickered tails and laughter's trace,
Shadows dance in playful grace.

In the twilight of a sibilant song,
Echoes linger, inviting the throng.
Whispers weave through the evening light,
Curious souls take flight in the night.

Colors blend in a mosaic swirl,
As starlit dreams begin to unfurl.
Each glimmer wraps the world in jest,
Enticing hearts to join the quest.

Those quirky shadows, bold and bright,
Roam through the silent hues of night.
With every twirl and pirouette,
The serpent smiles without regret.

Flora's Secrets in the Twilight Breeze

In the softness of a twilight haze,
Flora whispers of ancient ways.
Petals blush in the waning light,
Secrets shared with the coming night.

The wind carries tales on gentle sighs,
As leaves dance under twilight skies.
A tapestry of time unfolds,
In every bloom, a story told.

Golden threads of evening's grace,
Wrap around each flower's face.
With fragrant breaths, the night awakes,
In whispered notes, the heart partakes.

Each rustling leaf, a voice divine,
In the sacred hour, they intertwine.
With twilight's brush, they softly tease,
Unveiling life in the evening breeze.

Mystical Voices upon Emerald Shores

Where emerald waves kiss golden sand,
Mystical voices from sea to land.
In the cadence of the ocean's song,
Nature's chorus where dreams belong.

Echoes ring in the salty air,
Carried by currents, floating fair.
As twilight creeps across the sea,
Whispers flow, wild and free.

Stars awaken on the water's face,
Mirroring hearts in a timeless space.
Each ripple shares a forgotten tale,
Of love and loss in a fleeting gale.

The moonlight dances, shadows play,
In a serenade that bids the day.
Upon these shores where magic thrives,
The ocean sings, and the spirit strives.

Whispers of Color in the Glistening Grass

In fields awash with morning dew,
Whispers of color begin anew.
Each blade a canvas, vibrant and bright,
Painting dreams in the soft daylight.

The susurrus of petals in bloom,
Fills the air with sweet perfume.
Nature's palette, a feast for the eyes,
As hues mingle beneath vast skies.

From crimson reds to emerald greens,
Every shade tells of what it means.
Soft murmurs of life in the breeze,
Invite the heart to find its ease.

As whispers linger in the air,
Hidden wonders are waiting there.
In the glistening grass, we find our way,
Through colors that light the break of day.

Fragments of Daybreak in a Garden Dream

Within the garden, dawn breaks thin,
Soft light spills over petals pale,
Whispers of night start to rescind,
In gentle hues the shadows sail.

Birdsong flutters through the air,
Breezes dance along the ground,
Each flower awakened with care,
A symphony of silence found.

Butterflies grace the warm sunlight,
With wings adorned in colors bright,
They weave through blooms, a fleeting flight,
In this dream, all feels so right.

The dew-kissed leaves hold secrets shy,
Glistening like stars from the night,
Moments freeze as time slips by,
In beauty's grasp, pure delight.

As day unfolds in hues of gold,
Vibrant tales begin to weave,
In this garden, dreams are told,
Awake or lost, we still believe.

The Celestial Tapestry of Verdant Whispers

Beneath the sky, a canvas wide,
Green threads of life in harmony,
Each leaf a note, a voice inside,
Nature's song, a symphony.

Stars above wink with delight,
Night's cool breath caresses trees,
In this hush, the world feels right,
Filled with tales carried by the breeze.

Whispers linger among the blooms,
In hues of emerald, they sing,
Cradled softly, the night resumes,
A lullaby the shadows bring.

Every petal tells a story,
Of sunlit days and moonlit dreams,
In this dance, there's fleeting glory,
Life flows as sweet as flowing streams.

As dawn approaches, colors blend,
Golds and reds in gentle play,
In nature's arms, we find a friend,
In whispers, the night fades away.

Vibrant Echoes of the Secret Spring

Deep within the forest's heart,
Spring uncoils from icy grasp,
Life awakens, plants depart,
With each bloom, sweet moments clasp.

Crisp air carries scents anew,
Soft laughter echoes, bright and clear,
Colors burst, a vibrant view,
Nature whispers, "Spring is here."

Winding streams of crystal flow,
Reflecting skies of azure hue,
In this secret world, time's slow,
Every corner holds a clue.

The dance of petals on the ground,
Painting the earth in splendid hues,
In hidden spots, joys abound,
Awakening, the world renews.

Brightly crafted by the sun,
Joyful voices fill the air,
Spring's gentle hand has just begun,
In every heart, a secret rare.

Shadows Playing Among the Enchanted Blooms

In twilight's glow, shadows weave,
Among the petals, dark and light,
Whispers beckon, yet they leave,
A fleeting touch, a dream in flight.

Moonlight dances on the ground,
Casting patterns, soft and sweet,
With every rustle, secrets sound,
Hidden wonders, life's heartbeat.

Beneath the stars, flowers gleam,
As night unfolds its velvet shroud,
Each fragrant bloom, a whispered dream,
In silence, beauty feels so loud.

Mysteries linger in the air,
As gentle breezes touch the skin,
Soft laughter echoes everywhere,
In dusk's embrace, new tales begin.

Among the blooms, shadows play,
In playful waltz, they twirl and sway,
Life's fleeting moments softly stay,
As night transforms the end of day.

Hidden Colors in the Blooming Silhouettes

In gardens rich with hues so bright,
Petals whisper tales of light.
Beneath the sun, their secrets spun,
Hidden colors, grace begun.

A gentle breeze, a soft caress,
Wraps each bloom in tenderness.
In shadows deep, where dreams reside,
Nature's art cannot hide.

With vibrant strokes, the blossoms paint,
A masterpiece, both wild and quaint.
Each silhouette, a story told,
Of beauty, bold and uncontrolled.

From daffodils to roses fair,
They dance in sunlight, unaware.
Caught in time, they sway and twirl,
In the heart of a fragrant whirl.

So pause a moment, take a breath,
Embrace the colors, life's sweet depth.
In blooming silhouettes, we find,
The hidden hues that warm the mind.

Tales of the Verdant Fable

In emerald woods where soft wind sighs,
Nature spins its fable, wise.
Leaves fluttering, a dance of grace,
Echo stories in this place.

Beneath the canopy, shadows play,
Whispers of the night and day.
Each rustling branch a tale does weave,
Of life within, who dares believe.

The roots entwined in earth's embrace,
Hold secrets of a timeless space.
While flowers bloom in vibrant hues,
Each petal sings of morning dew.

With every step upon the ground,
Ancient echoes can be found.
Birds in song, a joyous tune,
Guided by the watchful moon.

So listen close, these tales unfold,
A verdant fable to be told.
Embrace the magic all around,
In nature's heart, our souls are bound.

Bubbles of Light Between the Petals

In gardens bright where shadows fade,
Bubbles of light begin to parade.
Dance like droplets on the breeze,
Whispers of joy in vibrant leaves.

Each flower holds a hidden glow,
Flickering softly, nature's flow.
Petals cradle these orbs of cheer,
Casting spells of love sincere.

Through fields adorned in lavender,
Bubbles rise and gently stir.
In the splendor of day's embrace,
Hope finds a home, a sacred space.

Glistening under the sun's warm kiss,
Moments cherished, purest bliss.
A fleeting dance, both sweet and brief,
In the bloom of light, we find relief.

So let the bubbles guide your way,
In the garden where dreams sway.
Innocent joys, a treasured sight,
Under the sun, so pure and bright.

The Mirthful Dance of the Painted Breeze

In twilight's glow, the breezes waltz,
With laughter light, they spin and haults.
Petals flutter in joyful grace,
As whispers trace this sacred space.

The colors swirl, a vivid sight,
As day gives way to tender night.
Each gust a brush, each sigh a song,
In nature's arms, we all belong.

With painted hues of sunset's sheen,
The breeze caresses where we've been.
In every twirl, in every laugh,
We find our peace, we find our path.

The dance unfolds in soft delight,
In every heartbeat, pure and bright.
The world a canvas, bold and free,
In the painted breeze, we long to be.

So let the mirthful winds embrace,
Every moment, every trace.
In this dance of life, we see,
The beauty held in harmony.

Chromatic Echoes in the Twilight Grove

In twilight's arms, the colors blend,
Where shadows dance and whispers send.
A symphony of huesplays anew,
As daylight fades to evening's dew.

Beneath the boughs, the spirits soar,
Painting dreams on ancient lore.
Each echo carries a gentle sigh,
In the grove where secrets lie.

The moonlight weaves a silver thread,
Caressing roots where fairies tread.
A tapestry of twilight's grace,
In Nature's arms, we find our place.

Stars illuminate the mystic scene,
Unveiling paths where we have been.
In shadows cast, the stories grow,
As chromatic echoes softly flow.

Shimmering Secrets of the Enchanted Meadow

In meadows bright, where whispers bloom,
Secrets shimmer, dispelling gloom.
Butterflies flit on gentle wings,
Carrying tales of forgotten things.

Each petal tells a story new,
Wrapped in hues of gold and blue.
Dance of the breeze, a tender sigh,
Underneath the vast expanse sky.

Moonbeams play on emerald grass,
As night unfolds, moments pass.
A tapestry of night's embrace,
In twinkling stars, we find our place.

The dew-kissed morn reveals delight,
Where dreams come alive in soft light.
In the meadow's heart, we roam free,
Shimmering secrets, just you and me.

Patterns of Light in the Whispering Leaves

In whispering leaves, soft patterns gleam,
Light dances gently, a fleeting dream.
Sunbeams trickle through leafy gates,
Creating art that nature creates.

The forest hums in rhythmic tones,
A symphony of whispered moans.
Every branch and every stem,
Leads us to a sacred gem.

Shadows flicker, a playful tease,
As sunlight kisses the ancient trees.
In this haven, time is still,
Echoes of magic, the heart to fill.

With every rustle, a story spun,
Patterns of light and shadows run.
In this glade, we find our way,
In whispered leaves, forever stay.

Fantasia of Colors and Shadows

In twilight's veil, a fantasia bright,
Colors dance in the fading light.
Each hue sings a melody sweet,
As shadows weave their gentle deceit.

Crimson reds and sapphire blues,
Merge in the sky, an artist's muse.
Beneath the stars, magic spins,
A carousel where the night begins.

Glimmers of gold on silken dreams,
Whispers of hope in moonlit beams.
Every color tells a tale,
In this enchanted, starlit trail.

The dance of the dusk, a symphony,
Filling the night with harmony.
In colors and shadows, we find bliss,
Fantasia lives in every kiss.

Mosaics of Color in a Whispering World

In quiet glades where shadows play,
Soft hues blend in the fading day.
Petals dance beneath the breeze,
Whispers carried through the trees.

Canvas strokes of light and shade,
In this world, a vibrant parade.
Golden threads of sunlight weave,
Nature's tapestry, we believe.

Crimson leaves and azure skies,
Mirror pools with secrets that rise.
Every glance reveals a tale,
In this splendor, hearts set sail.

The rustling grass, a gentle song,
Invites us to join and belong.
Each color tells a story true,
In whispers soft, the world renews.

Here time stands still, and peace is near,
In nature's arms, we lose all fear.
Mosaics bloom in silence bright,
A whispered world, a pure delight.

The Interwoven Canvas of Nature's Secrets

Threads of green twist and twine,
In this weave, the sun will shine.
Deer graze gently on meadow's edge,
Nature's secrets, a sacred pledge.

Rippled streams in hues of blue,
With each brush, a world anew.
Whispers echo through the trees,
A symphony carried by the breeze.

Fading echoes of bird songs sweet,
With every beat, our hearts compete.
Each blossom bright, a tale concealed,
In nature's arms, all is revealed.

In the distance, mountains hold,
Stories of the brave and bold.
Every shadow, every light,
Crafts the canvas, pure delight.

An interwoven melody plays,
Of sunlit dreams and twilight days.
Nature's secrets, softly spun,
In every drop, the dance begun.

Enchanted Murmurs in the Light of Day

In morning's glow, the world awakes,
A tapestry of light it makes.
Silhouettes in gold and green,
Enchanted whispers, softly seen.

Gentle breezes brush the trees,
Carrying tales with graceful ease.
Fairy wings in twilight's hue,
Every whisper speaks to you.

Sunbeams kiss the flowers' glow,
Painting paths where dreams can flow.
In every petal, secrets hide,
In nature's heart, pure joy resides.

Through forest paths where shadows dance,
Life unfolds in a sacred trance.
Enchanted murmurs fill the air,
Inviting souls to linger there.

As day unfolds, the magic swells,
In every echo, our heart dwells.
With every sigh, a wish takes flight,
In enchanted murmurs, pure delight.

The Garden of Echoing Colors

In the garden where colors bloom,
A symphony dispels the gloom.
Vibrant hues that dance and sway,
In nature's arms, they softly play.

Each petal holds a whispered dream,
As laughter blends with the sun's beam.
Among the blooms, we often find,
Echoes of a heart entwined.

Rustling leaves in laughter's jest,
Colors swirl, a lively fest.
Every shade a gentle sigh,
In the garden, we learn to fly.

Beneath the blooms, stories unfold,
In echoes of the brave and bold.
In fragrant air where sweetness lies,
Life's true beauty never dies.

As twilight casts its golden thread,
Colors whisper what once was said.
In the garden, our spirits soar,
Echoing colors forevermore.

Whimsical Tales in the Garden's Glow

In the garden where dreams reside,
Petals dance on a gentle tide.
Whispers of secrets softly flow,
Beneath the stars' enchanting glow.

Butterflies flit with joy in flight,
Crafting stories in morning light.
Each flower holds a tale to tell,
Of magic brewed in the petal's bell.

The moonlight weaves a silver thread,
Over paths where the fairies tread.
In shadows green, they play and twirl,
In a world of dreams, they joyfully swirl.

Crickets sing a lullaby sweet,
As blossoms bow, a floral feat.
With every breeze, a new tale spins,
In this garden where wonder begins.

So let your heart take flight and soar,
In the garden's tales forevermore.
Each moment cherished, a fleeting glance,
In the warmth of nature's dance.

Wandering Through Dappled Light and Shade

Beneath the trees, where shadows play,
I wander softly, come what may.
Sunlight dapples the earth below,
As time drifts by in a gentle flow.

The breeze carries laughter, light and free,
In this quiet space, just the trees and me.
Rustling leaves tell stories old,
Whispering secrets in hues of gold.

A path of petals leads my feet,
Through vibrant patches, a lively treat.
Each step unfolds a painted frame,
As nature dances, wild and untamed.

Illuminated moments brightly gleam,
In the heart of this wandering dream.
With every turn, a new delight,
Beneath the canopy's soft light.

So let me linger, lost in the shade,
Where every step is gently laid.
In the embrace of this tranquil glade,
I find my peace and never trade.

The Illumination of Forgotten Echoes

In the corridors of time, they speak,
Soft echoes rise from the shadowed peak.
Memories painted in hues so bright,
Awakening thoughts in the hush of night.

Whispers linger on the cool night air,
Tales of love and longing, laid bare.
Each echo glimmers, a fleeting jewel,
In the depths of silence, a hidden rule.

Tracing paths of the moments past,
Illuminated journeys that forever last.
Through the veil of time, they weave and blend,
A tapestry made, where memories mend.

In the stillness, the heart aligns,
With echoes that dance on the fragile lines.
Revealing stories that carve the soul,
Finding solace in the echoes' roll.

So let the past be a guiding light,
As echoes speak through the canvas of night.
In forgotten realms, may we grow,
Embracing the magic of all we know.

Mystical Reflections on Drifting Petals

Petals drift on a silken breeze,
Softly whispering through ancient trees.
In their descent, a story unfurls,
A kaleidoscope of colors swirls.

Each hue a sentiment, bright and bold,
Carved in nature's book of gold.
They paint the air with memories sweet,
As the earth cradles their gentle feat.

Reflecting the sun in a delicate dance,
In every flutter, a timeless chance.
To embrace the wonders that life bestows,
In a world of petals, anything goes.

Beneath the moon, their beauty glows,
Telling tales as the soft wind blows.
In whispered secrets, they spin and glide,
Each moment cherished, a joy-filled ride.

So let us gather these drifting dreams,
In a world where nothing is as it seems.
With petals as guides, we'll wander wide,
On mystical paths where heart resides.

The Dance of Whimsy on Emerald Paths

Beneath the sky of softest blue,
A breeze whispers secrets old and true.
With laughter light as dew on grass,
We twirl in moments, letting time pass.

The flowers sway in rhythmic grace,
Their colors bright, a warm embrace.
We chase the shadows, play in gleeful rift,
Each step a beat, a joyful gift.

In sunlit glades where dreams convene,
We weave our tales, both bold and serene.
With every turn, a story spins,
In this dance, where joy begins.

The emerald paths invite our souls,
Embracing freedom, making us whole.
With whimsy wrapped around our hearts,
Each fleeting moment, a work of art.

So let us dance till shadows claim,
This vibrant floor, our hearts aflame.
For in this waltz, nothing is lost,
In the dance of whimsy, we pay no cost.

Tapestry of Thoughts in Forgotten Spaces

In corners where the echoes sleep,
Thoughts drift gently, secrets to keep.
Weaving patterns, shadows unfold,
Stories linger, waiting to be told.

Amidst the dust, ideas rise,
Through tangled threads, we seek the wise.
Each fabric stained with colors bright,
Illustrates dreams born in the night.

With whispers soft, the memories stir,
A tapestry rich, emotions recur.
In forgotten spaces, we find the gold,
An inner journey, both brave and bold.

Fingers trace where silence dwells,
Listening closely to unspoken spells.
Each thread a pathway, each knot a chance,
Inviting the soul to join the dance.

So gather close, in shadows cast,
As we delve deep into the past.
In this tapestry, let thoughts entwine,
A woven journey, forever mine.

Ephemeral Lullabies Among Blooming Echoes

In gardens where the nightingale sings,
Soft lullabies on the breeze take wings.
Each note a whisper, sweetly spun,
Beneath the stars, our hearts are one.

Amidst the blooms, a fragrance lies,
Carrying dreams to the velvet skies.
Dancing petals with soft delight,
Echoing love through the quiet night.

Each moment fleeting, yet so profound,
In time's embrace, we are unbound.
With every sigh, a story flows,
In ephemeral dreams, our solace grows.

We gather light from the twilight hue,
As shadows weave through the petals' dew.
Lullabies born from a starlit glow,
Guide us gently where soft winds blow.

So close your eyes, let the echoes sway,
In blooming whispers, find your way.
For in this night, as dreams unfold,
Lies the magic of hearts untold.

Shifting Landscapes in Moonlight's Glow

In silver light, the world transforms,
Whispers of night in gentle swarms.
Mountains breathe and rivers gleam,
Awakening life from a gentle dream.

Each shadow dances, a waltz so sly,
As secrets linger in the starlit sky.
With every step, the ground will shift,
Transforming moments, nature's gift.

The moon's soft touch reveals the way,
Guiding lost souls till break of day.
In shifting landscapes, dreams collide,
Where wishes wander and love can hide.

A tapestry woven of night and light,
Paints the earth in colors bright.
With echoes of laughter, the journey flows,
In moonlight's glow, our wanderlust grows.

So let us roam till dawn descends,
With shifting paths that never end.
For in the night, our spirits soar,
In landscapes shifting, forevermore.

Spectrum Serenade on the Twilit Grass

The twilight dims, a soft embrace,
Colors blend in a tender trace.
Whispers echo through the night,
Nature's canvas, pure delight.

A breeze weaves tales in shades of blue,
Beneath the stars, a vibrant hue.
Moonlight dances, shadows play,
In this peace, the heart will stay.

Deer step lightly, a gentle sigh,
Fireflies flicker, as dreams fly high.
The crickets sing their twilight tune,
Harmonies rise beneath the moon.

Each moment held in twilight's grasp,
Fleeting beauty in dreams we clasp.
Colors whisper, secrets shared,
In every breath, the soul is bared.

As dawn approaches, shadows fade,
Yet in the heart, the colors played.
A spectrum soft, a serenade,
In twilit grass, our joys arrayed.

Voices of the Chromatic Wildflowers

In fields where colors brightly bloom,
Wildflowers sing, dispelling gloom.
Petals sway in the gentle breeze,
Whispers sweet as honeyed bees.

Scarlet poppies shout their cheer,
Daisies dance, while the sun draws near.
Lilacs hum in vibrant throng,
Nature's voices weave a song.

Amongst the hues, a story's told,
Of sun and rain, of young and old.
Each blossom sways, with spirits bright,
Collective joy in pure sunlight.

A tapestry of fragrant dreams,
Of laughter, hope, and silent screams.
Each flower tells a tale unknown,
In their silence, wisdom grown.

As twilight edges close the day,
The colors fade, but memories stay.
In the whispers of night, they'll sing,
Voices of wildflowers take wing.

The Enigma of the Prismatic Glade

In a glade where secrets lie,
Colors pulse beneath the sky.
Shadows twine with beams of light,
Mysteries breathe, both day and night.

Crimson leaves in autumns pass,
Emerald grasses, the dreamer's glass.
Golden rays weave through the trees,
Echoes linger on the breeze.

Here, the stillness speaks so loud,
Wrapped in an ethereal shroud.
Time stands still in this embrace,
Every moment, a fleeting grace.

Sapphire lakes reflect the mind,
In their depths, what truths we find?
Silent guardians of the glade,
Where thoughts converge and dreams are laid.

With every sunset, colors blend,
The enigma, where wonders end.
In prismatic shades, minds take flight,
Lost in brilliance, hearts ignite.

Rhythms of the Colorful Serenade

Underneath the vivid sky,
Colors clash, as rhythms fly.
Echoes of the vibrant dawn,
A symphony of hues is drawn.

Dancing shadows, soft refrain,
In the light, all joy remains.
Every brush of color bold,
Spins a tale, a joy retold.

As petals flutter, spirits rise,
In the breeze, a sweet surprise.
Nature's orchestra, pure and free,
Conducts the heart's own melody.

From morning bloom to twilight's end,
Colors weave, and time will bend.
In every note, a world unfurls,
Rhythms of life in colorful swirls.

As night descends, hues softly blend,
A serenade that will not end.
In dreams, the colors shall parade,
In every heart, a vibrant glade.

Vibrancy of Life in Thicket's Embrace

In thicket's heart, where shadows play,
Life unfolds in a wild ballet.
Birds chirp bright, in leafy nooks,
Nature's canvas, rich as books.

Flowers bloom in colors bold,
Whispers of warmth in marigold.
Breezes dance through budding trees,
A symphony carried on the breeze.

Squirrels scamper, swift and spry,
Underneath the vast blue sky.
Sunlight filters, golden rays,
In this vibrant, green-filled maze.

Life entwined in roots so deep,
Hidden secrets, nature's keep.
Emerald hues paint every lane,
No moment lost, in joy or rain.

The thicket thrives, a tale untold,
In its embrace, both wild and bold.
Here in nature, heart takes flight,
Vibrancy glows, day and night.

Shifting Colors of an Autumnal Dream

Leaves descend in swirling grace,
Painting earth in a warm embrace.
Crisp air whispers tales of change,
A vibrant world, both vast and strange.

Gold and amber, russet hues,
In every shade, a tale renews.
Pumpkin patches dot the land,
Harvest charm, so finely planned.

Winds carry scents of sweet decay,
The golden hour fades to gray.
Branches bare against the sky,
Nature's canvas, breathing sighs.

Fires crackle with warm delight,
Gathered close, our spirits bright.
Stories shared beneath the moon,
Autumn's song, a gentle tune.

Ephemeral, this fleeting sight,
Colors shifting, day to night.
In dreams of fall, we find our way,
A tapestry in shades of clay.

Enchanted Secrets of the Whispering Trees

In twilight's hush, the trees confide,
Secrets echo, path aside.
Branches sway, with stories spun,
Echoes of a thousand suns.

Mossy blankets, soft and green,
A hidden world, serene, unseen.
Leaves murmur tales of ages past,
In their whispers, shadows cast.

Roots entwined in ancient lore,
Between the trunks lies so much more.
Eyes of deer peer through the brush,
Nature's quiet, elegant hush.

Moonlight weaves through every limb,
In every breeze, a gentle hymn.
Magic lingers, thick and sweet,
Underneath the stars, we meet.

Boundless beauty in the night,
Whispers hold both grace and fright.
Tales of wonder, old and wise,
In the trees, our dreams arise.

The Renaissance of Shades in the Dragon's Lair

Deep in the lair where legends sleep,
Colors awaken, secrets keep.
Flickering flames dance on stone,
In shadows deep, the bravest roam.

Emerald greens and sapphire blues,
Sparkling gems in ancient hues.
Glimmers of gold that tell a tale,
Of whispered winds in dragon's trail.

Mystic realms where dreams collide,
In the cave where shadows bide.
Light reflects on rugged walls,
Echoing the ancient calls.

Breath of fire, a radiant glow,
Casting spells on all below.
In this haven, dark yet bright,
The renaissance of sheer delight.

Tales of glory rise and fall,
Within the lair, they softly call.
Shades of wonder, fierce and rare,
In the heartbeats of the air.

Chromatic Dances Among Whispering Petals

In fields where colors swirl and sway,
The petals whisper secrets bright,
A dance of hues in soft ballet,
As day dissolves into the night.

Beneath the arch of twilight's veil,
The blossoms shimmer, pulse, and gleam,
Through fragrant air, their stories sail,
Like fleeting shadows in a dream.

The breeze, it weaves a gentle tune,
Where rose and lavender entwine,
Beneath the watchful, silver moon,
In harmony, their hearts align.

A canvas vast, an artist's dream,
With shades of love and joy imbued,
In every fold, emotions teem,
A world reborn, forever renewed.

As dawn arrives, the colors fade,
Yet still the echoes linger near,
A memory, a serenade,
In chromatic dances, crystal clear.

The Language of Light in the Garden of Dreams

In gardens where the shadows play,
The light unveils a secret song,
Each leaf and petal finds their way,
To join a chorus, pure and strong.

A whisper of the morning dew,
Invites the sun to take its stand,
And gilds the blooms in gold anew,
While time slips softly through our hands.

The colors shift with every breath,
A dance of rays that intertwine,
Through twilight's grace, we glimpse a myth,
The magic of the divine design.

In every corner, stories gleam,
Of hopes and dreams, both near and far,
The language spoken in a beam,
That leads us where our wishes are.

As night enfolds the garden tight,
The stars ignite the dreamer's muse,
In tender beams, they share their light,
Revealing paths we dare to choose.

Saffron Skies Above the Emerald Tides

Where saffron skies embrace the seas,
And emerald waves caress the shore,
A tapestry of nature's tease,
Invites the heart to seek for more.

The sun dips low, a molten sphere,
It paints the horizon with fervent glow,
A moment's peace, the world so dear,
In whispers soft, the breezes flow.

With every wave, a story told,
Of journeys vast and dreams untamed,
The tides, they dance, both shy and bold,
In rhythms wild, yet unashamed.

As twilight beckons, colors clash,
The saffron fades to dusky hues,
A fleeting glimpse, a vibrant flash,
As day surrenders to night's muse.

And in this realm of shifting skies,
Where emerald cliffs meet sapphire waves,
The heart can soar, the spirit flies,
In nature's arms, the soul is saved.

Elysian Whispers of Pastel Mornings

In pastel realms where silence reigns,
The morning light creeps softly near,
With whispers sweet that break the chains,
Of night's cool grasp, so calm and clear.

Each blossom wakes with gentle grace,
A symphony of colors blend,
As nature paints a warm embrace,
To greet the day, to start anew.

The dew-kissed grass reflects the sun,
While birds in chorus lift their song,
In this serene, enchanted run,
The world feels right, where all belong.

A canvas stretches, vast and wide,
Where dreams can merge with waking thoughts,
In every corner, joy can hide,
Awaiting hearts, in peace, it rots.

As shadows stretch and morning glows,
The whispers linger, soft and bright,
In Elysian fields, the spirit knows,
A realm of beauty kissed by light.

Radiant Journeys in the Whispering Wilds

In twilight's glow, the shadows dance,
Beneath the stars, we seize the chance.
Paths unfold through fragrant air,
Each whisper leads us, unaware.

Golden rays break through the trees,
Rustling leaves, a gentle breeze.
Feet upon the mossy ground,
In nature's haven, peace is found.

With each step, the world does sigh,
Silent wonders passing by.
In the wild, our spirits soar,
Radiant journeys to explore.

Moonlit streams that gently flow,
Guiding us where dreams will grow.
Underneath the night's embrace,
We find our joy, our secret place.

The whispering wildcalls to our hearts,
A tapestry of nature and art.
Hand in hand, we roam so free,
In radiant journeys, just you and me.

Echoes of Enchantment Beneath Ferns

Beneath the ferns, a soft refrain,
Nature hums an ancient gain.
Echoes of magic fill the air,
Whispers of dreams, beyond compare.

In moonlit glades, shadows entwine,
With every step, the world aligns.
Glimmers of light on dewy leaves,
A symphony that never leaves.

The gentle touch of time stands still,
In this haven, hearts can thrill.
Rustling whispers, secret songs,
Each moment here, where we belong.

Fairy tales in every breeze,
A dance of magic through the trees.
Beneath the ferns, a world so vast,
In enchantment's arms, we are cast.

The forest sings, its heart exposed,
In echoes, our wonder grows.
Tales of wonder now ignite,
Beneath the ferns, in soft twilight.

Spectrum of Secrets in the Garden's Song

In gardens bright, where colors bloom,
A spectrum thrives, dispelling gloom.
Whispers linger among the petals,
Secrets held in nature's settles.

Each flower tells a tale so sweet,
With fragrant hints, our senses greet.
Butterflies weave through sunlit air,
In this haven, dreams lay bare.

Paths lined with hope, in hues so bold,
Stories of life and love retold.
The garden hums, a gentle song,
In every note, we both belong.

With every breeze, the magic flows,
In sunset's glow, the beauty grows.
Spectrum of secrets, we unveil,
In each whisper, we set sail.

Holding hands, we dance through time,
In this symphony, life's pure rhyme.
In the garden's song, we find our way,
Unfolding dreams of yesterday.

Dreamlike Sojourn in Serene Landscapes

In tranquil fields, the wildflowers sway,
A dreamlike sojourn, we find our way.
Beneath the vast and starry skies,
Serene landscapes where time softly flies.

With every step, our spirits rise,
In harmony with nature's sighs.
Gentle streams that laugh and play,
Whispers of night beckon to stay.

The hills embrace us, calm and bright,
In solace found among the light.
Mountains stand in silence proud,
In dreamlike visions, unbowed.

Fields of gold beneath the sun,
In every heartbeat, we are one.
Waves of peace forever flow,
In these serene realms, our hearts will grow.

With dreams that linger, hand in hand,
We wander through this sacred land.
In every breath, the world reclaims,
A sojourn timeless, free of chains.

Chromatic Echoes in the Garden's Heart

In the garden's quiet hum,
Colors dance and softly come.
Petals whisper tales of light,
As day surrenders into night.

Butterflies flit with gentle grace,
Tracing patterns, leaving no trace.
Shadows weave in the golden hue,
Life's tapestry, vibrant and true.

Fragrant blooms in fragrant air,
Hope and dreams linger everywhere.
A symphony of scents so rare,
Nature's wonder, beyond compare.

Rustling leaves in breezy sighs,
Carry echoes of whispered ties.
Sunset paints the world in gold,
Secrets of the earth unfolds.

In this realm of vivid grace,
Time pauses in a dance, a space.
Chromatic echoes softly blend,
As garden's heart shall never end.

Enigmatic Murmurs under Celestial Vines

Beneath the stars, the vines entwine,
In shadows deep, their secrets shine.
Voices whisper soft and low,
Tales of worlds we long to know.

Moonlight bathes the leaves in silver,
As night unveils the heart's deep quiver.
Beats of nature pulse the air,
Enigmatic murmurs linger there.

Cool winds carry a soothing tune,
Guiding dreams beneath the moon.
Starlit paths where thoughts can roam,
Awakening the soul's true home.

Tangled roots with stories vast,
Linking futures to the past.
In this haven, whispers speak,
A language ancient, soft yet sleek.

Here in twilight's gentle embrace,
We find solace, space, and grace.
Celestial vines our fears release,
In murmurs, we discover peace.

Vibrant Dreams Amongst the Reeds

Amongst the reeds, where waters flow,
Vivid dreams in colors grow.
Spirits dance with nature's chime,
In rhythm, weaving threads of time.

Whispers rise with the morning breeze,
Carrying tales from distant seas.
Golden rays of sun ignite,
Awakening the world in light.

Rippling waters, stories told,
Of wanderers, both young and old.
Reflections shimmer, hopes take flight,
Vibrant dreams in pure delight.

The rushes sway, a soft ballet,
Guiding thoughts that slip away.
Here, in nature's gentle clasp,
We learn to dream, to love, to grasp.

In the hush of evening's hue,
We'll chase the stars, the night anew.
Amongst the reeds, our spirits beam,
In vibrant dreams, we find our theme.

Whirling Colors Beneath the Ancient Oak

Beneath the oak, where ages blend,
Whirling colors never end.
Leaves that twirl in breezy flight,
A canvas splashed with pure delight.

Roots that drink from earth so deep,
Guarding secrets lost in sleep.
With every breeze, the whispers call,
Inviting us to share it all.

Sunrise paints with amber glow,
Transforming life in vibrant flow.
Each moment spun in hues so bright,
In nature's arms, all hearts take flight.

As shadows dance with evening's grace,
Nightfall brings a soft embrace.
By ancient oak, where spirits play,
We find our dreams in night and day.

In this realm, time bends and sways,
Eternal echoes fill our days.
Whirling colors, hearts entwined,
Underneath the oak, peace we find.

Echoes of the Past in a Verdant Realm

In whispers of leaves, the stories unfold,
Nestled in roots, where memories hold.
Time drifts like shadows beneath ancient trees,
Each rustle a tale, carried by the breeze.

Footprints of old in the soft, mossy ground,
Echoes of laughter, a warmth all around.
In the stillness of dusk, secrets take flight,
As stars twinkle softly, embracing the night.

Crystal clear streams that shimmer with grace,
Mirroring whispers of the past's embrace.
Nature's embrace wraps the heart with a song,
In a verdant realm where our souls still belong.

The pulse of the earth, a beat long retained,
Stories of love, of joy, and of pain.
With each gentle rustle, the ancients take part,
Echoes resounding through the depths of the heart.

A tapestry woven with threads of the past,
In shadows and sunlight, forever they'll last.
Within every leaf, and each petal's sigh,
Echoes of history whisper and fly.

Velvet Hues in Morning's Breath

Morning unfurls with a soft, gentle glow,
Wrapping the world in a warm, sweet tableau.
Velvet hues dance upon petals of light,
Awakening dreams to take graceful flight.

The sky blushes softly, as sun kisses dew,
Nature's embrace feels fresh, vibrant, anew.
Colors cascade like a tender embrace,
In morning's breath, life finds its own place.

Whispers of color in blossoms arise,
As gold meets the lilac in softening skies.
Each moment a canvas, a fleeting delight,
Woven together in soft morning's light.

Birdsongs awaken the shimmering sheen,
Nature's orchestra playing, serene yet keen.
Velvet dreams dance through the whispering grass,
As shadows retreat and the moments amass.

In dawn's tender embrace, hopes brightly unfurl,
Colors of life like a precious pearl.
With each golden ray, the world comes alive,
In velvet hues, the soul learns to thrive.

Secret Pathways of Colors in Twilight

Twilight descends with a soft, gentle sigh,
Colors entwined in the indigo sky.
Secret pathways of dusk gently unfold,
A tapestry woven in violet and gold.

Whispers of darkness meet light in a dance,
Shadows elongate in a twilight romance.
Silhouettes sway like the dreams of the night,
A journey through colors, a wondrous sight.

In hidden corners where the soft petals sleep,
Mysteries linger in silence so deep.
The stars begin twinkling, a glittering trace,
Mapping the journeys of those who embrace.

Embers of twilight, enchanting and rare,
Colors awaken in the cool evening air.
Pathways emerge beneath the deepening hue,
Leading our hearts where the dreams feel renewed.

In secret, the twilight cradles the day,
Painting the night with a gentle bouquet.
Colors unite in an elegant swirl,
As shadows and light in harmony twirl.

The Hidden Symphony of Nature's Brush

In valleys and hills, a whispering call,
Nature's soft symphony, echoing all.
With each gentle stroke, the landscape ignites,
An artist at work, crafting day into nights.

Brushes of wind sweep through meadows so wide,
Painting the petals with grace as they glide.
Scenes filled with color, like dreams left to flow,
Framing each moment with beauty aglow.

The rustling leaves form a melody sweet,
As footsteps of critters create nature's beat.
In the dance of the branches, a songbird will croon,
Harmonizing whispers beneath the full moon.

Each color a note in a symphonic play,
The heartbeat of nature guides night into day.
With every brushstroke, the world comes alive,
In this hidden symphony where dreams strive to thrive.

As twilight brushes the landscape to sleep,
A chorus of crickets quietly creep.
In the stillness, the magic is spun,
The hidden symphony, where all life is one.